AL-GHAZZALI ON THE TREATMENT OF PRIDE AND CONCEIT

Ḥujjat al-Islām Abū Ḥāmid
Muḥammad Ghazzālī Ṭūsī

TRANSLATED FROM THE PERSIAN BY
MUHAMMAD NUR ABDUS SALAM

INTRODUCTION BY
LALEH BAKHTIAR

SERIES EDITOR
SEYYED HOSSEIN NASR

GREAT BOOKS OF THE ISLAMIC WORLD

2 *Alchemy of Happpiness*

© 2002 Great Books of the Islamic World, Inc.
All rights reserved. No part of this book may be reproduced, stored in a retrieval system, or transmitted, in any form or by any means, electronic, mechanical, photocopying, recording or otherwise, without the written permission of the publishers.

Library of Congress Cataloging-in-Publication Data

Ḥujjat al-Islām Abū Ḥāmid Muḥammad Ghazzālī Ṭūsī (AH450/CE1059 to AH505/CE1111), commonly known as al-Ghazzali. *Al-Ghazzali On the Treatment of Pride and Conceit* from the *Alchemy of Happiness (Kimiya al-saadat)*, the Persian translation by al-Ghazzali of the *Ihya ulum al-din (Revival of the Religious Sciences)*
  1. Islamic psychology. 2. Sufism. 3. Islamic theology—Early works to 1800. 4. Ghazzali, 1058-1111. I. Title.

ISBN: 1-57644-702-3 pbk

Cover design: Liaquat Ali
  Cornerstones are Allah and Muhammad connected by *Bismillāh al-Raḥmān al-Raḥīm* (In the Name of God, the Merciful, the Compassionate).

Logo design by Mani Ardalan Farhadi
  The cypress tree bending with the wind, the source for the paisley design, is a symbol of the perfect Muslim, who, as the tree, bends with the wind of God's Will.

Published by
Great Books of the Islamic World, Inc.
Distributed by
KAZI Publications, Inc.
3023 W. Belmont Avenue
Chicago IL 60618
Tel: 773-267-7001; FAX: 773-267-7002
email: info@kazi.org /www.kazi.org

INTRODUCTION

"... be not like those who forgot God and [eventually] God caused them to forget their 'self'... " (Q. 59:18-19)

There is nothing more timely today than a translation of the remarkable work on Islam of al-Ghazzali for two reasons. First of all, the results of recent studies of medicine-psychology and religious belief[1] confirm that the religious model works in the healing process so traditional wisdom must be made available in English for all researchers as well as readers to be able to access it and draw upon it for areas of further research. Secondly, at a time when the world is confused by the varying beliefs of Muslims and are interested in studying what the majority of the world's Muslims believe, the works of al-Ghazzali provide the perfect opportunity.

Abu Hamid Muhammad al-Ghazzali was born in the city of Tus, northwestern Iran, in AD 1058.[2] He studied in Tus until he was twenty-seven when he moved to Baghdad. He was appointed as a professor at the Nizamiyyah college there when he was thirty-three. After four years of a strenuous schedule, he underwent a spiritual experience which convinced him that all of the knowledge he had gained was useless in comparison to gnosis or experiential knowledge of the Divine Presence. He realized unless he left his position and was free to search for this knowledge deeper within himself

4 Alchemy of Happpiness

without worldly distractions, he would never attain it. He therefore provided for his family and left for Damascus and other well known cities at that time.

When he was forty-eight he returned to his birthplace where he lived for the next five years until his early death at the age of fifty-three.[3] He left behind over 400 works among them being his famous *Revival of the Religious Sciences* (*Ihya ulum al-din*) which he wrote in Arabic. Over 2300 pages, it is a compendium of Islamic practices. A few years after he finished the *Revival*, he felt the need to write the same sort of compendium on being a Muslim in Persian. This is the entire work here translated into English for the first time which al-Ghazzali called the *Alchemy of Happiness*. It is a masterful textbook on traditional psychology.[4]

While modern Western psychology focuses on describing emotions, behavior or cognition, that is, what we feel, do and think without recourse to the basic principles or causes, traditional psychology is based on the same three centers, but like all traditional sciences, includes much more. As a result of including metaphysics, theology, cosmology and the natural sciences as the basis or underlying principles for what we feel, do or think, it becomes a wholistic psychology. The goal of traditional psychology is to assume the noble character traits, to overcome our ego which competes for our attention with our God-given instinct to attend to the One God. In this view, there cannot be two wills and therefore our free will has to be disciplined to submit to God's will (*islam*).

The word psychology comes from the Greek words "psyche" or "soul" and "logos." Psyche also means breath, spirit and refers to the animating principle of the universe. Logos means "word" and in the traditional view it refers to "the Word of God." The science of psychology, then, when it is true to its name, is the study of the Word of God within the human soul or spirit.

Al-Ghazzali's psychology is essentially that of monotheism and unity, the world view that "there is no god, but God" or "there is no deity, but God." It is to see the universe and all that is in it as aspects of the One God. The world view of monotheism (*tawhid*) forms the underlying basis for traditional psychology.

By the word "tradition" we mean *al-din* which has been defined as: "truths or principles of a Divine Origin revealed or unveiled to mankind through a messenger along with the ramifications and application of these principles in different realms including law, social structure, art, symbols, the sciences and embracing Supreme Knowledge along with the means for its attainment."[5]

Tradition (*al-din*) is a point which is at one and the same time the Center and Origin of our being. Traditional psychology is oriented towards helping the individual as well as the human community find that Center as we prepare for the return to our Origin.

A monotheist (*hanif*) like al-Ghazzali regards the whole universe as a unity, as a single form, a single living and conscious thing, possessing will, intelligence, feeling, and purpose, revolving in a just and orderly system in which there is no discrimination no matter what one's gender, color, race, class, or faith be. All comes from God and returns to God, while a multitheist (*mushrik*) views the universe as a discordant assemblage full of disunity, contradiction, and heterogeneity containing many independent and conflicting poles, unconnected desires, customs, purposes, wills, sexes, sects, colors, races, classes, and faiths.

The monotheistic world view sees the universal unity in existence, a unity of three separate relationships: (1) our relationship with others, nature and the universe; (2) our relationship with God; (3) our relationship with our "self." These relationships are not alien to one another; there are no boundaries between them. They move in the same direction. Al-Ghazzali expresses this when he writes:

> Then know that there is a station in gnosis (*marifat*) where, when a person reaches it, he really sees that all that exists is interconnectedness, one with another, and all are like one animate being. The relationship of the parts of the world such as the heavens, the earth, the stars to each other is like the relationship of the parts of one animate being to each other. The relationship of all the world to its Director—from one aspect, not from all aspects—is like the relationship of the kingdom of the body of an animal to the spirit and intellect which are its Director. Until a person recognizes this, that Verily, God created Adam in His image, it cannot be comprehended by his understanding."[6]

Other non-monotheistic religious world views see the Divinity—or even the plural of this—as existing in a special, metaphysical world of the gods, a higher world as contrasted with the lower world of nature and matter. They teach that God is separate from the world, created it and then left it alone. In the monotheistic world view, God has never left and is the destination of the Return. In this view, our "self" fears only one Power and is answerable to only one Judge; turns to one direction (*qiblah*), orienting all hopes and desires to only one Source. A belief in monotheism gives us a sense of independence and liberation from everything other than God and a connectedness to the universe and all that it contains. Submission to God's Will alone liberates us from worshipping anything other than God and rebelling against anything else that purports to be God.

AL-GHAZZALI'S THREE FUNDAMENTALS

Al-Ghazzali sees the basis for traditional psychology leading to self-development as consisting of three fundamentals—the same three fundamentals confirmed by modern psychology and scientific studies—affect, behavior and cognition (the ABC of psychology). The first fundamental is knowledge (cognition, awareness or consciousness). The second he calls states (affect or emotion) that that knowledge or awareness produces in us. The third he calls act or deed— the action that results from our emotion that came from our knowledge or awareness of something.

THE FIRST FUNDAMENTAL: KNOWLEDGE
(COGNITION)

According to al-Ghazzali, knowledge should be used to come to understand the articles of belief rather than accepting them on faith alone. The articles of belief include: the belief that God is One; the belief that God sent Prophets to guide mankind to Him and that Muhammad (ﷺ) is the Messenger and last Prophet who will be sent (until the end of time when Jesus (ﷺ) will return) and that the Quran is the last revelation; the belief in angels and the Scriptures; and the belief that after death we will be resurrected in the Hereafter and judged by God who will reward or punish us depending upon our intentions. Al-Ghazzali says: "It is the states of the heart, the place of our intentions, that holds us accountable."[7]

BELIEFS

Our beliefs are the guiding principles that give meaning and direction to our life. They filter our perceptions of the world. When we freely choose to believe something is true, a command is delivered to our spiritual heart (mind) telling us how to represent what we have come to believe to be true. When the process has been accomplished with Divine Grace (defined by al-Ghazzali as: the harmony, agreement and concord of our will and action with God's will), our beliefs can become our most effective force for creating the positive and good in our lives.

In explaining the importance of coming to the realization of the Oneness of God oneself and not accepting it because someone has told us, al-Ghazzali says:

> Know that the first duty incumbent upon whoever becomes a Muslim is to know and believe the meaning of the utterance "there is no god but God, Muhammad is the Messenger of God," which he pronounces with his tongue, understands in his heart, and believes so that he entertains no doubt about it. When he has believed and his heart is established firmly upon (that belief)—so that doubt cannot touch it—it is sufficient for the basis of being (one who submits to God's Will (*muslim*)). Knowing it with evidence and proof is an individual duty incumbent upon every (one who submits to God's Will (*muslim*)). The Prophet (ﷺ) did not command the Arabs to seek proofs, to study theology, or to look for doubts and replies to those; rather, he was content with belief and faith.[8]

He then defines what belief in submission to God's Will (*islam*) means:

> Know that you have been created and that you have a Creator Who is the Creator of all the universe and all that it contains. He is One. He has no partner nor associate. He is Unique, for He has no peer. He always was; His existence has no beginning. He always shall be; there is no end to His existence. His existence in eternity and infinity is a necessary, for annihilation cannot touch Him. His existence is by His own essence. He needs nothing but nothing is unneedful of Him. Rather, He is estab-

lished by His Own essence, and everything else is established through Him.[9]

Al-Ghazzali mentions five sources for our beliefs:

(1) Our environment: how we grow up; models of success or failure we learn from; what is right and what is wrong; what is possible and what is impossible.

(2) Our experiences and events as we grow up.

(3) Knowledge: what we know and do not know; that we continue to educate our "self" from "the cradle to the grave."

(4) Results we have seen achieved in the past, learned from the stories of past people in the Quran.

(5) Setting new goals to achieve future results.

Future results depend upon how we incorporate our beliefs—how we view the world—into our own self image. According to al-Ghazzali, our firm and certain belief in the Oneness of God should lead us—as it did Prophet Muhammad (ﷺ)—to the following beliefs:

(i) The belief that everything happens for a reason. We look for the good and positive in whatever happens.

(ii) The belief that there is no such thing as failure, only results or outcomes. If we are able to train a falcon to hunt for us, al-Ghazzali uses as an example, we can train and discipline our rational faculty to control our passions. Al-Ghazzali says that we should not expect immediate results. Change is gradual. We need to develop patience, a great virtue in his view.

(iii) The belief that we must take responsibility for whatever happens. No matter what happens, know and believe that we are in charge. The Prophet never blamed others for whatever happened. He never allowed himself to be a victim. As the Quran says: "*God does not change the condition of a people until they change what is within themselves.*" (Q. 13:11)

(iv) The belief that we need to learn from other people who

are our greatest resource. Treat them with respect and dignity as the Prophet did.

(v) The belief that we need to challenge our profession or line of work and excel in it. Explore new ways of doing things. Increase our sense of curiosity and vitality.

(vi) The belief that there is no success without commitment. Know our outcome in the Hereafter as the Prophet knew. Develop our sensory responses so we know what we are getting and then continue to refine it until we get what we want. Study the key beliefs of the Prophet and then hold tight to them.

In al-Ghazzali's view, if we firmly believe we are among those "who submit to God's Will" (*muslim*), then with our cognition, affect and behavior as understood from the monotheistic point of view as our foundation, we can submit in everything that we say or do. What we believe to be true becomes possible when we know what we want—to be one who submits to God's will—and believe we can achieve it.

STRATEGIES

Developing a strategy is to duplicate our belief system. When we organize the way we think, the way we feel and the way we behave according to our belief system, we have developed a strategy. The ingredients of our strategy are our human experiences. Our experiences are fed from our five outer senses: seeing, smelling, hearing, tasting and touching. Our five senses motivate us to action. When we are aware of what they perceive and keep their perceptions in line with our belief system, we have developed a successful strategy.

The amounts we use of the information provided by our senses is monitored by our spiritual heart (mind). Are the images small or large, bright or unclear, close up or far away? How we put these together, their order and sequence clarifies our strategy.

With our resource being our "self" consisting of body, spirit, soul and spiritual heart (it is our spiritual heart that centers us), we want to learn what we need to do to organize this resource. How can we have our goal and belief achieve the greatest potential? What is the most effective way to use the resource of our "self" and its subparts? The most effective strategy has always been modeling the behavior of others who have the same goal and the same belief. For the believer, this model is that of the Messenger Muhammad (ﷺ) who was the perfect human being.

Strategies he used included performing the prescribed fast as well as formal prayer, supplication and continuous recitation of the revelation. For the believer, revelation brought both a Law and a Way. Both serve as strategies of how to approach life in the manner in which the model approached life, and knowing that our model did not always do things exactly the same way.

The strategy of Quranic recitation is yet another form of discipline. One of the verses of the Quran: *"Remember Me and I will remember you,"* (Q. 2:152) makes this form of supplication a very rich traditional strategy to attain spiritual energy.

THE SECOND FUNDAMENTAL: STATES
(AFFECT, EMOTION)

Our belief establishes states (emotions, affect) which then result in our actions. In this relationship and all others, our state of mind is
important because that determines our emotion and our emotion determines how many resources are available to us. Our emotions depend upon how we feel physically—our breathing, posture, etc.— and how we represent the world to ourselves internally. When we have cleared our spiritual heart of hypocrisy in our acts of worship, our actions are to worship

God and we are at the beginning stages of the greater struggle according to al-Ghazzali.

States (affect, emotion) are held or transformed in terms of psychology through moral values that energize us. Our behavior is the result of the state we are in at the time. Our emotional state governors our behavior. Behavior is the result of how we represent the information from our senses internally as well as our muscular tension, posture, physiology.

We have the resources we need to succeed. We have to learn how to access them. We need to learn to take direct control: Once we learn to manage our states (emotions), according to al-Ghazzali, we can modify our behavior. There is a difference of how people react to the same state. The difference depends on their model.

One of the best methods which al-Ghazzali uses over and over again in the *Alchemy* is that of what is today called reframing: changing the way we evaluate what something means. If our culture teaches us that change is a failure of opportunity for learning, we need to become resourceful, to realize that nothing has power over us but the power we give it by our own conscious thoughts. The meaning of any experience depends on the frame we put around it. If we change the context or reference point, the process changes.

We can reframe by context reframing or content reframing. With context reframing, we take a bad experience and show it in another way. With content reframing, we drastically change how we see, hear, or represent a situation. We learn to change the way we represent a situation so we feel differently about it. Now we are at the level of choice instead of reaction. By learning to reframe, we change our emotions so that they empower us. We can either associate or disassociate. If we associate consciously, we learn to change the way we represent things, thereby changing our behavior. We have to aim for congruence between our spiritual heart (mind) and body.

Al-Ghazzali On Treating Pride and Co

CLARITY OF MORAL VALUES

Clarity of values gives us a sense of who we are and why we do what we do. If we have an internal conflict between our values and our strategy, we will not succeed. Values determine what really matters in life. They provide us with a basis from which to make sound judgments about what makes life worth living.

Al-Ghazzali refers to verses 23:1-10 of the Quran as an example of believers who have succeeded by incorporating Quranic values:

> Certainly will the believers have succeeded: They who during their prayer humbly submissive; those who turn away from ill speech; they who are observant of the poor-due; they who guard their private parts except from their wives and those their right hands possess for indeed, they will not be blamed, but whatever seeks beyond that, then they are the transgressors; and they who are to their trusts and their promises attentive; and they who carefully maintain their prayers. Those are the inheritors. (Q. 23:1-10)

Al-Ghazzali then summarizes the verses to describe a person of good character.

> A person of good character is he who is modest, says little, causes little trouble, speaks the truth, seeks the good, worships much, has few faults, meddles little, desires the good for all, and does good works for all. He is compassionate, dignified, measured, patient, content, grateful, sympathetic, friendly, abstinent, and not greedy. He does not use foul language, nor does he exhibit haste, nor does he harbor hatred in his heart. He is not envious. He is candid, well-spoken, and his friendship and

enmity, his anger and his pleasure are for the sake of God Most High and nothing more.[10]

In the *Alchemy* (as well as in the *Revival*), al-Ghazzali devotes the major part of the work to clarity of moral values by describing in great detail what he calls the Destroyers and the Deliverers. He not only describes them in each of those parts, but offers treatment as to how to get rid of them (the Destroyers) or how to incorporate them into our personality (the Deliverers). Doing this clarifies the moral values of the one who submits to God's Will.

As a result of the performance of the acts of worship, if accompanied by Divine Grace, the one who submits to the Will of God will be receptive to the adoption of positive dispositions (the deliverers) like temperance, courage, wisdom, and justice and be able to avoid negative dispositions (the destroyers) like anger, fear of other than God, cowardice, lust, envy, apathy, preconsciousness (knowing that you do not know), unconsciousness (not knowing that you do not know) and overconsciousness (knowing but deceiving the self about it), but only on the condition that others benefit from the positive dispositions one has attained. This, then, makes it encumbent on the one who has submitted to the Will of God to come to know and act upon the commands that underlie the relationship of self to others.

Energy

The entire human organism is a complete system that makes use of energy transformed from food and air to satisfy its various natural dispositions. Perception (external and internal senses) and motivation develop, according to traditional psychology, from the animal soul. Motivation is the seat of impulses towards inclinations which are imprinted on the external or internal senses and then, through filtering into what is called the practical intellect (the mind), a response is given. Three energy sources are active in this perspective: natural (venial, *tabiiya*), vital (arterial, *nafsaniyah*), and nervous (*hawaniyah*). These transformed energies are distributed throughout the body. The heart is considered to be the point of contact between the energy of the body and that of the self.

Without the necessary energy, which according to al-Ghazzali comes from spiritual practices, we reach a state of hoplessness and despair. For instance, if someone asked: "If one has been condemned to hardship, what is the benefit of the greater struggle?" Al-Ghazzali explains this attitude:

> Your question is valid. These words are correct in that they are the cause of the illness of our heart. That is, when a sign of a concept that a person has been condemned to hardship falls upon his heart, they cause him to make no effort, neither sowing nor reaping. Such a sign would be when a person who has been condemned to death becomes hungry the thought occurs in his heart not to eat. He says: "What good is bread to me?" He does not extend his hand to eat and he does not eat until by necessity he dies. If he has been condemned to poverty, he says: "Of what use is sowing seed?" so he neither sows nor reaps. And he for whom happiness has been decreed, he has been made aware that wealth and life have been decreed for him. They have been decreed because he has cultivated, done business, and consumed. Therefore, this decree is not invalid; rather it has reasons"[11]

THE THIRD FUNDAMENTAL: ACTIONS (BEHAVIOR)

Knowledge alone is not sufficient for we who accepted the trusteeship of nature and were endowed with the Divine Spirit which includes our abilities to choose, to discern, and to gain consciousness of our "self." It is through actions based on knowledge that the centered self benefits another as proof of being centered. The major pillars include ritual purity (*taharah*) and ritual prayer (*salah*), ritual fast (*saum*), the paying of the alms tax (*zakah*), the pilgrimage (*hajj*), counseling to positive dispositions and preventing the development of negative ones (*amr bil maruf wa nahy an al-munkar*) and *jihad* or struggle in the Way of God, the greater struggle of which is the inward struggle of the self (*jihad al-akbar*). The last two are the major concern of traditional psychology.

BONDING POWER OR RAPPORT

Bonding and communicating are aspects of action—proof of the extent of transformation through attaining the goal that we had intended. The power to bond with others is an extraordinary human power. It comes in the true sense when bonding develops from the heart and not from either the intellect or the passions. It comes from a deep love for one's fellow human being and arises when we try to meet the needs of others before our own needs, much like a mother with her new born child.

Al-Ghazzali quoting from the Quran, the Prophet and the Companions mentions how important it is to eat with other people and to perform the formal obligatory prayer with other people.

COMMUNICATORS

Believers should conceivably be master communicators on all three levels—with self, with others and with the Source. How we communicate determines the quality of our lives. Through spiritual disciplines like, for example, prescribed fasting, believers are given an opportunity, a challenge. If they are able to communicate that challenge to themselves successfully, they will find the ability to change. This is not to accept prescribed fasting as only a religious duty but rather as a divine challenge, as a chance for growth instead of an experience which limits self. In this way we will become master communicators because our very life will communicate our vision, goal and beliefs to others to help them change for the better, as well.

RELATIONSHIP TO OTHERS

Al-Ghazzali discusses knowledge (cognition), states (affect) and action (behavior) in three relationships: our relationship with others; our relationship with our Creator-Guide; and our relationship with our "self."

The model for this is the *sunnah* of Muhammad (ﷺ) who said, "I was sent to complete the noble qualities of dispositions," explaining that God loves the positive dispositions and not the negative ones. Al-Ghazzali also quotes another Tradition in this regard, "By Him in whose hand is my life, no one shall enter paradise except the one who has positive dispositions." Al-Ghazzali says, "God taught [Muhammad (ﷺ)] all the fine qualities of disposition, praiseworthy paths, reports about the first and last affairs, and matters through which one achieves salvation and reward in future life and happiness and reward in the world to come."

Quoting the Traditions, al-Ghazzali shows the relationship established by the Prophet with others.

> And the Messenger (ﷺ) said: "There are not two persons who love each other for the sake of God that the one most beloved by God is the one loves the other the most." And he (ﷺ) said: "God Most High says: 'My love is a right for those who visit one another for My sake, who love each other for My sake, who are generous to each other with their

wealth for My sake, and who aid each other for My sake.'" And he (ﷺ) said: "On the Day of Resurrection God Most High will say: 'Where are those persons who loved each other for My sake so that I may keep them in My shadow on this day when there is no shade for the people in which to take refuge?'" And he (ﷺ) said: "There are seven persons on the Day of Resurrection who, when there will be no shade for anyone, will be in the shadow of God Most High: the just leader (imam), the young person who began worshipping God Most High at the beginning of his youth, the man who leaves the mosque with his heart attached to the mosque until he returns to it again, two people who love each other for the sake of God Most High and who come together for that and separate for that, the person who remembers God Most High in private and whose eyes fill with tears, and the man who when called by a magnificent and beautiful woman says to her: 'I fear God Most High,' and the man who gives voluntary charity with his right hand so that the left hand has knowledge of it." And he (ﷺ) said: "No one visits a brother for the sake of God Most High save that an angel cries out, saying: 'Be happy and blessed! Thine is the heaven of God Most High!'"

And he (ﷺ) said: "A man was going to visit a friend. God Most High sent an angel in his path who asked: 'Where are you going?' He replied: 'To visit such-and-such a brother.' (The angel) asked: 'Do you have some business with him?' He said: 'No.' (The angel) asked: 'Are you related to him in some way?' He said: 'No.' (The angel) asked: 'Has he done something good for you?' He answered: 'No.' (The angel) said: 'Then why are you going to him?' He answered: 'I love him for the sake of God.' (The angel) said: 'Then, God Most High has sent me to you to give you the good news that God Most High loves you because of your love for him, and has made heaven an obligation for both of you yourselves.'" And the Messenger (ﷺ) said: "The strongest resort of faith is love and enmity for the sake of God Most High."[12]

Al-Ghazzali describes relationships with others ranking them in degrees.

> The first degree is that you love someone for some reason linked with him, but that motive is religious and for the sake of God Most High; as you like your teacher because he teaches you knowledge. That friendship is of a divine nature since your aim for (acquiring) this knowledge is the Hereafter, not rank or wealth. If the object be the world, that friendship is not of that kind. If you love your student so that he learn from you and may obtain the pleasure of God Most High through learning, (you) too obtain the spiritual reward of teaching. This is for the sake of God Most High. But if you love (him) for the sake of dignity and retinue, it will not be of that kind. If a person gives voluntary charity and likes a person on the condition that he deliver that to the poor; or he invites some poor people and likes a person who prepares a good meal, then such friendship is for the sake of God. Indeed, if one likes someone and gives him bread and clothing to give him the leisure to worship (God), it is friendship for the sake of God, since his motive is the peace of mind for worship.
> Many religious scholars and worshippers have had friendships with the rich and powerful for this reason. Both were counted as friends for the sake of God Most High. Moreover, if one loves his own wife because she keeps him from corruption and because of the bringing forth of children who will supplicate for him, such love is for the sake of God Most High and everything you spent for her is a voluntary

charity. Indeed, if one loves his student for two reasons: one that he serves him and the other that he gives him the peace of mind to perform his worship, that part which is for worship is counted as love for the sake of God most High and there is spiritual reward for it.

The second degree is greater. It is that one love a person for the sake of God without having any expectations from him; instead, it is by reason of obedience to God and for the love of Him that he loves the other. Moreover, because he is a servant of God and created by Him—such friendship is divine. It is greater because this arises from the excess of one's love of God Most High, so much so that it reaches the boundaries of passionate love. Whoever is in love with someone, loves (that person's) district and neighborhood. He loves the walls of (that person's) house; indeed, he loves the dog roaming the quarter's streets, and he likes that dog more than other (dogs). He is compelled to love the friend of his beloved, and beloved of his beloved, the people who obey the commands of his beloved; (the beloved's) servants, captives, or relatives; all of these he loves out of necessity, for his love spreads to whatever has a relation with his beloved. As his love increases so it does with the others who follow and are connected with the beloved.[13]

ESTABLISHING THE RELATIONSHIP
BETWEEN THE SELF AND OUR CREATOR-GUIDE

This relationship is established, according to al-Ghazzali, through the commands of worship (*ibadah*), which are the most fundamental means of communication between our "self" and God. They embody the same three aspects: knowledge (cognition), states (affect, process) and action (behavior). One who submits to the Will of God seeks knowledge of particular guidance. This produces a "state" (emotion) in the self which then responds with an action as al-Ghazzali explains:

> Know that object and kernel of all acts of worship are the remembrance of God Most High; that the buttress of Islam is obligatory formal prayer, the object of which is the remembrance of God Most High. As He said: *Surely (formal) prayer prevents lewdness and evil, and indeed the remembrance of God is greater (than all else).* (Q. 29:45)
>
> Reading the Quran is the most meritorious of the acts of worship, for the reason that it is the word of God Most High: (reading or reciting it) is remembering Him. Everything that is in it all cause a renewal of the remembrance of God, may He be praised and exalted. The object of fasting is the reduction of the carnal appetite so that the heart, liberated from the annoyance of the carnal appetites, becomes purified and the abode of remembrance; for when the heart is filled with carnal appetite, it is not possible to remember (Him); nor does (the remembrance) affect one. The object of the greater pilgrimage, which is a visit to the House of God, is the remembrance of the Lord of that House and the incitement of longing for meeting Him.
>
> Thus the inner mystery and the kernel of all of the acts of worship are remembrance. Indeed, the basis of Islam is the declaration: "there is no god but God"; this is the source of remembrance. All other acts of worship stress this remembrance. God's remembrance of you is the fruit of your remembrance of Him; what fruit could be greater than this? For this He said: *So remember Me, I shall remember you.* (Q. 2:152)
>
> This remembrance must be continuous. If it is not continuous, it should be most of the time; for salvation is tied to it. For this He said: *And remember God much; perhaps you will be successful.* (Q. 62:10) He says that if you have the hope of salva-

tion, the key to that is much remembrance, not a little, and more frequently, not less.

And for this He said: *Those who remember God standing, sitting, and lying down.* (Q. 3:191) He praised these people because they do not neglect (remembrance) standing, sitting, lying down, or in any condition. And He said: *Remember thy Lord, (O Muhammad), within thyself humbly and with awe, in a soft voice, in the morning and in the evening, and be not of the neglectful.* (Q. 7:205) He said: "*Remember Him with weeping, fear, and in concealment, morning and evening, and do not neglect (this) at any time.*"

The Messenger (ﷺ) was asked: "What is the best of acts?" He answered: "That you die with your tongue moist with the remembrance of God Most High." And he said: "Should I not inform you of the best of your actions—the most acceptable to the King, may He be exalted—and your highest degrees, that which is better than giving alms of silver and gold, and better than shedding your blood in battle against enemies in defense of the faith?" They asked: "What is that, O Messenger of God?" He said: "The remembrance of God." The remembrance of God Most High! And he said: "Whoever remembering me engages in worshipful supplication of God, his gift is, in my opinion, greater and better than giving (charity) to beggars." And he said: "The rememberer of God Most High among the heedless is like a living person amongst the dead, or like a green tree amongst dead vegetation, or like the warrior for the faith who stands fighting amongst those fleeing. . .[14] In summary, the strength of one's love for God Most High is in accordance with the strength of one's faith. The stronger one's faith, the more overwhelming one's love is.[15]

Know Your "Self"

The most important relationship for the purposes of traditional psychology is that of our relationship to our "self." Our "self" as we have seen, consists of body, spirit, soul and spiritual heart. We turn now to the *Alchemy*'s Prolegomena (added here by al-Ghazzali, it does not appear in the *Revival*) where al-Ghazzali explores how to come to know the "self" in great detail.

*****

The traditional method of teaching a text is for the teacher to read it part by part with a class of students and then comment on what the text is saying. This is the method used next taking just the first subsection of Topic One of the Prolegomena, "Knowing Yourself" which appears in the following paragraphs in bold. The commentary and explanations that follow are enhanced with other sections of al-Ghazzali's writings in the *Alchemy* which are inset for clarity. If we were sitting in al-Ghazzali's classroom, this is the method he would be using.

Notes to the Introduction

1 See works like *Timeless Healing: The Power and Biology of Belief* by Herbert Benson; *Why God Won't Go Away: Brain Science and the Biology of Belief* by Andrew Newberg, Eugene D'Aquili and Vince Rause; and *Handbook of Religion and Health* edited by Harold G. Koniz, Michael McCullough and David B. Larsen.

2 Other well known writers and poets born in Tus include Abu Yazid Bistami, Husayn bin Mansur Hallaj, Abu Said Abi'l-Khayr, Nizam al-Mulk, Firdawsi and Umar Khayyam.

3 See Bibliography to the Introduction for the numerous books that detail the life of al-Ghazzali. It is interesting to note that al-Ghazzali wrote the *Alchemy of Happiness* when the First Crusade ruled Jerusalem. Saladin arrived on the scene seventy-seven years after al-Ghazzali's death.

4 See below for the definition of traditional psychology which historically was called the science of ethics or practical wisdom (*hikmat al-amali*).

5 *Knowledge and the Sacred*, p. 68.

6 *Alchemy*, p. 841.

7 This is a clear distinction with modern secular psychology which is limited to only treating a human being part by part instead of holistically. See *Alchemy* p 817.

8 *Alchemy*, p 358.

9 *Alchemy*, p. 116.

10 *Alchemy*, p 525.

11 *Alchemy*, p 780.

12 *Alchemy*, p 358.

13 *Alchemy*, p 360.

14 *Alchemy*, pp 221-222.

15 *Ibid*.

BIBLIOGRAPHY

Al-Ghazzali On Disciplining the Self. Translated from the *Alchemy of Happiness* by Muhammad Nur (Jay R. Crook). Chicago: Kazi Publications, 2002.

al-Ghazzali. *On Disciplining the Soul and the Two Desires.* Translated from the *Ihya ulum al-din (Kitab riyadat al-nafs. Kitab kasr al-shahwatayn)* by T. J. Winter. Cambridge: Islamic Texts Society, 2001.

al-Ghazzali. *On Divine Predicates and their Properties (al-Iqtisad fil'itiqad).* Translated by Abdu Rahman Abu Zayd. India: Kitab Bhavan, 1994.

Al-Ghazzali On Earning a Living and Trade. Translated from *Alchemy of Happiness* by Muhammad Nur (Jay R. Crook). Chicago: Kazi Publications, 2002.

Al-Ghazzali On Enjoining Good and Forbidding Wrong. Translated from *Alchemy of Happiness* by Muhammad Nur (Jay R. Crook). Chicago: Kazi Publications, 2002.

Al-Ghazzali On Governing and Managing the State. Translated from *Alchemy of Happiness* by Muhammad Nur (Jay R. Crook). Chicago: Kazi Publications, 2002.

Al-Ghazzali On Hope and Fear. Translated from *Alchemy of Happiness* by Muhammad Nur (Jay R. Crook). Chicago: Kazi Publications, 2002.

Al-Ghazzali On Journeying. Translated from *Alchemy of Happiness* by Muhammad Nur (Jay R. Crook). Chicago: Kazi Publications, 2002.

Al-Ghazzali On Knowing This World and the Hereafter. Translated from *Alchemy of Happiness* by Muhammad Nur (Jay R. Crook). Chicago: Kazi Publications, 2002.

Al-Ghazzali On Knowing Yourself and God. Translated from *Alchemy of Happiness* by Muhammad Nur (Jay R. Crook). Chicago: Kazi Publications, 2002.

Al-Ghazzali On Listening to Music. Translated from *Alchemy of Happiness* by Muhammad Nur (Jay R. Crook). Chicago: Kazi Publications, 2002.

Al-Ghazzali On Love, Longing and Contentment. Translated from *Alchemy of Happiness* by Muhammad Nur (Jay R. Crook). Chicago: Kazi Publications, 2002.

Al-Ghazzali On Marriage. Translated from *Alchemy of Happiness* by Muhammad Nur (Jay R. Crook). Chicago: Kazi Publications, 2002.

Al-Ghazzali On Meditation. Translated from *Alchemy of Happiness* by Muhammad Nur (Jay R. Crook). Chicago: Kazi Publications, 2002.

Al-Ghazzali On Patience and Gratitude. Translated from *Alchemy of Happiness* by Muhammad Nur (Jay R. Crook). Chicago: Kazi Publications, 2002.

Al-Ghazzali On Reckoning and Guarding. Translated from *Alchemy of*

Happiness by Muhammad Nur (Jay R. Crook). Chicago: Kazi Publications, 2002.

Al-Ghazzali On Remembering Death and the States of the Hereafter. Translated from *Alchemy of Happiness* by Muhammad Nur (Jay R. Crook). Chicago: Kazi Publications, 2002.

Al-Ghazzali On Repentance. Translated from *Alchemy of Happiness* by Muhammad Nur (Jay R. Crook). Chicago: Kazi Publications, 2002.

Al-Ghazzali On Spiritual Poverty and Asceticism. Translated from *Alchemy of Happiness* by Muhammad Nur (Jay R. Crook). Chicago: Kazi Publications, 2002.

Al-Ghazzali On Sufism. Translated from *Alchemy of Happiness* by Muhammad Nur (Jay R. Crook). Chicago: Kazi Publications, 2002.

Al-Ghazzali On the Duties of Brotherhood. Translated from *Alchemy of Happiness* by Muhammad Nur (Jay R. Crook). Chicago: Kazi Publications, 2002.

Al-Ghazzali On the Etiquette of Eating. Translated from *Alchemy of Happiness* by Muhammad Nur (Jay R. Crook). Chicago: Kazi Publications, 2002.

al-Ghazzali. *On the Foundations of the Articles of Faith*. Translated from the *Ihya ulum al-din (Kitab qawaid al-aqaid)* by Nabih Amir Faris. Lahore: Sh. Muhammad Ashraf, 1999.

Al-Ghazzali On the Lawful, the Unlawful and the Doubtful. Translated from *Alchemy of Happiness* by Muhammad Nur (Jay R. Crook). Chicago: Kazi Publications, 2002.

al-Ghazzali. *On the Manners Relating to Eating*. Translated from the *Ihya ulum al-din (Kitab adab al-akl)* by D. Johnson-Davies. Cambridge: Islamic Texts Society, 2000.

Al-Ghazzali On the Mysteries of the Pillars of Islam. Translated from *Alchemy of Happiness* by Muhammad Nur (Jay R. Crook). Chicago: Kazi Publications, 2002.

Al-Ghazzali On the Treatment of Anger, Hatred and Envy. Translated from *Alchemy of Happiness* by Muhammad Nur (Jay R. Crook). Chicago: Kazi Publications, 2002.

Al-Ghazzali On the Treatment of Hypocrisy. Translated from *Alchemy of Happiness* by Muhammad Nur (Jay R. Crook). Chicago: Kazi Publications, 2002.

Al-Ghazzali On the Treatment of Ignorance Arising from Heedlessness, Error and Delusion. Translated from *Alchemy of Happiness* by Muhammad Nur (Jay R. Crook). Chicago: Kazi Publications, 2002.

Al-Ghazzali On the Treatment of Love for This World. Translated from *Alchemy of Happiness* by Muhammad Nur (Jay R. Crook). Chicago: Kazi Publications, 2002.

AL-GHAZZALI ON THE TREATMENT OF PRIDE AND CONCEIT

Know that pride and self-importance are blameworthy traits and, in fact, enmity to God, may He be praise and exalted; magnificence and grandeur are appropriate only for Him. For this reason there are many reproaches for the tyrant and the arrogant in the Quran, as when He said: *Thus doth God print on every arrogant, disdainful heart.* (Q. 40:35) And He said: *Then was disappointed every obdurate tyrant.* (Q. 14:15) And He said through the voice of Moses (ﷺ): *"Lo! I seek refuge in my Lord and your Lord from every scorner who believes not in a Day of Reckoning."* (Q. 40:27)

The Messenger (ﷺ) said: "A person will not enter heaven who has in his heart pride in the amount of a grain or a mustard seed." And he (ﷺ) said: "There are people who make a business of self-importance until their names are recorded in the ledger of the tyrannical. They will receive the same punishment as (the tyrants) do."

In the Traditions it is related that Solomon (ﷺ) commanded all the satans, *jinn*, fowl of the air, and mankind to come out. Two-hundred thousand people and two-hundred thousand *jinn* assembled upon his carpet. He commanded the wind to lift it and carry it close to the sky so that they could hear the voices of angels and their glorifications. It landed upon the earth so as to reach the depths of the sea. At that moment he heard a voice: "If there were one atom of pride in the heart of Solomon, I would have swallowed him up in the earth before I would have taken him into the air."

The Messenger (ﷺ) said: "The arrogant will be gathered on the Day of Resurrection in the shape of ants beneath the people's feet, so despised are they by God Most High." And he (ﷺ) said: "There is a valley in hell called Habhab. It is right for God Most High to place the arrogant there." Salman Farsi, may God be pleased with him, said: "The sin for which no act of devotion has any profit is pride."

The Messenger (ﷺ) said: "God Most High will not look at a person whose clothing drags on the ground in the way of arrogance and swaggering in pride." And he (ﷺ) said: "Once a man was strutting and admiring his magnificent garments. God Most High had him swallowed into the earth and he is still there, until the Resurrection." And he said: "Whoever magnifies himself and struts upon the earth sees God Most High's anger at him on the Day of Resurrection."

Muhammad bin Wasi once saw his own son swaggering. He called him and said: "Do you have any idea who you are? I bought your mother with 200 dirhams and among the Muslims your father is such that the fewer like him there are, the better!" Mutarrif bin Abd Allah saw Muhallib strutting about. He said: "Captive! God Most High holds such a manner of going in enmity." (Muhallib) replied: "Beware! Do you know me?" He answered: "I know you: first you were a putrid fluid and at the end (you will be) an infamous corpse; in between, (you are) the carrier of pollutions."

1 THE VIRTUE OF HUMILITY

The Messenger (ﷺ) said: "No one has behaved with humility whose honor God Most High did not increase." And he (ﷺ) said: "There is no person whose head does not have reins held by the hands of two angels. When he shows humility, the reins are pulled upward and they say: 'O Lord God! Exalt him!' If he shows haughtiness, they drag his head down and say: 'O Lord God! Disgrace him!'" And he (ﷺ) said: "Blessed is that person who behaves humbly not out of desperation, who spends the wealth he has accumulated not in sin, who shows mercy upon the helpless, and who converses with the wise and learned."

Abu Salamah Madani tells of his grandfather who said: "Once the Messenger (ﷺ) was our guest while he was fasting. We brought him a cup of milk for his breaking of the fast. When he tasted it and found it sweet, he asked: 'What is this?' We said: 'We have mixed honey in it.' He set it down and did not drink it, saying: 'I do not say that it is forbidden, but whoever is humble for the sake of God Most High, God Most High exalts him and gives him eminence; whoever is proud God Most High throws down and despises; whoever spends in moderation God Most High makes self-sufficient; whoever spends immoderately God makes a pauper; whoever remembers God Most High often, God Most High takes as His friend."

Once a poor man with sores came to the door of the Messenger (ﷺ) and begged. The Messenger (ﷺ) was eating; he called him in and drew him to himself. The Messenger (ﷺ) sat him against his own thigh and said: "Eat." One of the Quraysh deemed the man filthy and looked upon him with dislike; he did not die before being afflicted with the same calamity.

The Messenger (ﷺ) said: "God Most High gave me the choice between being a messenger as a servant or being a king as a prophet. I hesitated in this and my friend among the angels, Gabriel, was present and I looked to him. He said: 'Humble yourself before God Most High.' I said: 'I desire to be a servant and a messenger.'" God Most High revealed to Moses (ﷺ): "I accept the formal prayer of the person who is humble and is not arrogant with My people and whose heart holds fear; he passes the day in the remembrance of Me and holds himself from (his) carnal appetites for My sake." And the

Messenger (ﷺ) said: "Nobility lies in piety, honor lies in humility, and riches lie in certainty."

Jesus (﷽) said: "Blessed are the humble of this world for they shall be the possessors of the pulpits at the Resurrection; blessed are the persons who make peace among people in this world for their place shall be in Paradise; blessed are the person whose hearts are unsullied by the world, for seeing God Most High shall be their spiritual reward."

Said the Messenger (ﷺ): "Whomever God Most High has shown the path to Islam, He has created in a good form and He has not made his condition such that He would be ashamed of him. Even though He has mixed his sustenance with humbleness, to God Most High he is one of the chosen."

Someone had prominent pock marks and some people were eating. Whomever he sat beside would get up and move off. The Messenger (ﷺ) showed him to a place close to himself and said: "I like very much the person who takes his necessities in his hand and carries them to his home. They are the provisions for his family. For this reason pride departs from him." And he (ﷺ) said to the Companions: "Why is that I do not see the sweetness of worship upon you?" They asked: "What is the sweetness of worship?" He answered: "Humility." And he (ﷺ) said: "Whenever you see a humble person be humble with him; when you see the prideful, be proud so that their affront and baseness may be revealed."

(1) NON-PROPHETIC TRADITIONS

Ayishah, may God be pleased with her, says: "You are neglectful of the most excellent act of worship and that is humility." Fudayl, may God have mercy upon him, said: "Humility is that you accept truth from whoever it is, even a child or the most ignorant of people." Ibn al-Mubarak, may God be pleased with him, says: "Humility is that you consider

Al-Ghazzali On Treating Pride and Conceit

yourself lower than whoever has fewer of the things of the world than you do so as to show him that you do not give yourself any value because of the worldly goods, and that you consider yourself above anyone who has more of the world than you so as to show him that he has no value to you because of his worldly goods."

God Most High revealed to Jesus (ﷺ): "Whenever I send you a comfort, if you come before that humbly, I shall perfect that comfort upon you." Ibn Sammak, may God have mercy upon him used to say to Harun al-Rashid every day: "O Commander of the Believers! Your humility lies is in your honor; it is more honorable that honor." (Harun) said: "You have spoken very well." Then (Ibn Sammak) said: "O Commander of the Believers! To whomever God Most High has given wealth, beauty, and retinue and who does good with that wealth, is humble amidst his retinue, and is abstemious in his beauty; his name is recorded in the ledger of God Most High among the pure." Harun called for pen and paper and wrote down those words. Solomon (ﷺ) used to enquire of the rich in his kingdom in the morning, then he would sit with the poor. He used to say: "I am a pauper, a pauper as much as you."

Some of the saints have spoken about humility:

Hasan Basri, may God be pleased with him, said: "Humility is that when you come out of your house you see no one whom you do not consider superior to yourself." Malik bin Dinar, may God be pleased with him, said: "If they cry from the top of the gate of the mosque: 'Let the worst of you come out,' no one will get himself in front of me, except by force." Ibn Mubarak heard this; he said: "The greatness of Malik was due to this." Someone came to Shibli, may God have mercy upon him. (Shibli) asked: "What are you?" He answered: "I am that dot which is placed under (the letter) '*b*'; that is, there is nothing lower than I." (Shibli) said: "May God destroy thy self-interest! May God carry off your self from before you, for you have caused your self to alight in another place!" One of the saints saw Ali, may God be pleased with him, in a dream. He asked him to give him advice: He said: "How good is the humility of the rich before the poor for sake of the spiritual reward of the Hereafter; how much better is the pride of the poor, confident of the grace of God Most High, with the rich."

Yahya bin Khalid, may God be pleased with him, says: "When a generous person becomes pious, he becomes humble; when the fool or the ignoble becomes pious, arrogance appears in him." Bayazid, may God have mercy upon him, says: "Until a servant (of God) considers no person worse than himself, he is prideful." One day Junayd said during the Friday assembly: "If it were not in the Traditions that at the end of time the elders of the people would be the most ignoble of them, I would not consider it right to address the congregation." Junayd, may God have mercy upon him, says: "To the people of the Unity of God, humility is pride; that is, humility is that one lower oneself, and since there is a need to keep low; one places one's self in a place so that one may then lower (oneself)." Whenever there was a wind or thunder, Ata-yi Sullami, may God have mercy upon him, would rise and, placing his hands on his belly like a pregnant woman, say: "Ah! That which comes upon people is all because of my inauspiciousness." Some people bragged in the presence of Salman. He said: "My beginning is a clot (of semen) and my end is carrion; then the worse from the better will appear at the scales, and the noble from the ignoble which is I."

2 THE TRUTH OF PRIDE AND ITS HARM

Know that pride is a trait of character, and character is an attribute of the heart, but its effect becomes evident on the exterior. The characteristic of pride is that one holds oneself before others and considers oneself better; from this a joyous puffing up appears in him. That puffing up which appears in him is called "pride." The Messenger (ﷺ) said: "I seek refuge with Thee from the puffing up of pride." When this puffing up appears in him, he considers others less than himself and looks upon them as servants. It may be that he not recognized his own servants and say: "Who may you be to be fit to serve me?" Just as the caliphs do not grant permission for everyone to kiss their threshold, nor do they write "(your) servant," except to kings. This is the ultimate pride and reaches the grandeur of God Most High, for He receives everyone in (their) servitude and prostration. If one does not reach that level, he seeks precedence in going and sitting; he expects respect. It gets to the point where if he is advised, he does not accept it; but when he himself gives advice, he speaks harshly. If he is instructed, he becomes angry. He looks upon people as he looks upon beasts.

The Messenger (ﷺ) was asked: "What is pride?" He replied: "That one does not submit to God and one looks upon people with contempt." These two traits are heavy veils between one and God Most High. From them all unseemly traits of character are born and one remains deprived of all good traits. Whoever is conquered by lordship, self-love, and self-importance cannot approve of that which he approves of for himself for the Muslims—-and this is not the way of the believers—and cannot humble himself with another—and this is not the attribute of the pious. He cannot restrain his animus and envy; he cannot swallow his anger; he cannot withhold his tongue from backbiting, nor can he cleanse his heart from deceit and spite, for his heart is seized by hatred for anyone who does not bow to him.

The least of this is that he is engaged daily with self-adoration and self-promotion. He does not omit fraud, lies, and hypocrisy in order to promote himself in the eyes of people.

The truth is that no one smells the perfume of being a Muslim so long as he does not forget himself; indeed, neither does he obtain the ease of the world. One of the saints said: "If you wish to smell the scent of heaven, consider yourself lower than all mankind so as to smell the scent of heaven."

If a person is granted the vision to see what is inside the hearts of those two arrogant persons when they meet, there is not in any dunghill the stench and ignominy which is in their hearts. Internally, they have the shapes of dogs and externally they adorn themselves as do women. They do not possess that companionability which Muslims have when they sit together. Indeed, you find tranquillity when your totality is lost in whomever you see, and all becomes homage to him, until duality departs. He remains and you do not remain, or he is lost in you and you remain but he does not; or both of yourselves are lost in God Most High, and you do not pay attention to yourselves. This is perfection. Perfection will necessarily come from this singularity. In sum, as long as there is duality, there can be no tranquillity. Tranquillity lies in the Oneness (of God) and singularity. This is the truth of pride and its harm.

3 THE DEGREES OF PRIDE

Know that some kinds of pride are more flagrant and greater than others; the difference arises from the fact that arrogance has three aspects: with respect to God Most High, the Messenger (ﷺ), or people.

(1) The first (degree) is arrogance with respect to God Most High, such as the pride of Nimrod, Pharaoh, and Iblis, and those who have claimed divinity, and (those who) have considered servitude to God Most High demeaning. God Most High said: *The Messiah will never scorn to be a servant of God,*

nor will the angels who are near (to Him). (Q. 4:172) Neither Jesus (ﷺ) nor the nearest angels disdain serving (God).

(2) The second degree is arrogance with respect to the Messenger of God Most High, such as the unbelieving Quraysh who said: *"We shall not bow to a person like ourselves. Why is an angel not sent to us?"* Or: *"Why was someone powerful not sent? An orphan was sent!"* And they say: *'If only this Quran had been revealed to some great man of the two towns!'* (Q. 43:31) They were of two groups: for one group their pride became a veil so that they did not ponder and did not recognize his Messengership; as when He said: *I shall turn away from My revelations those who magnify themselves wrongfully in the earth.* (Q. 7:146) He said: *"I shall permit the proud to see the signs of truth."* Another group knew, but rejected him; because of their pride, they could not bring themselves to admit it, as when He said: *And they denied (the signs), though their souls acknowledged them, out of spite and arrogance.* (Q. 27:14)

(3) The third degree is that one be haughty with other servants (of God) and look upon them with contempt. He does not concede their rights and considers himself better than they and puffs himself up. This, even though it is lower than the other two degrees, is nonetheless important for two reasons:

One is that greatness is an attribute of God Most High; a weak helpless man has nothing of his affair in his own hands. Where does greatness come from that a person (dare) consider himself its possessor? If he thinks himself great, he contends with God Most High in His attributes. He is like the captive who places a royal crown upon his head and sits upon a throne. Look at how deserving of loathing and punishment he becomes! Concerning this, God Most High said: Greatness is a loin cloth and majesty a robe; I have shattered whoever vies with Me in these two (attributes). He said: "Greatness and majesty are My special attributes. I shall destroy whoever vies with Me in them." So, since pride over (His) servants is not fitting for anyone save the Creator, if one of His servants is overbearing to Him, he will have competed with Him, just as when someone commands the personal captives of the king, which is not proper for anyone other than the king.

(4) Another reason is that this pride is an obstacle preventing the acceptance of truth from others. When a people have this trait, they dispute about questions of religion. When the truth appears on the tongue of one, pride prompts the other to deny it and not to accept it. These are the traits of the hypocrites and the unbelievers, as God Most High said concerning the unbelievers: Those who disbelieve say: *'Heed not this Quran, and drown out the hearing of it; haply ye may prevail.'* (Q. 41:26) And as He said: *And when it is said to him: "Be careful of thy duty to God, pride takes him to sin.* (Q. 2:206) When it is said to one: "Fear God Most High," he says: "Mind your own business." One time the Messenger (ﷺ) said to someone: "Eat with your right hand." (The other) replied: "I cannot." (The Messenger) said: "May he not be able to do it!" for he knew that the man had spoken out of pride. His hand became limp so that it no longer moved.

Know that the story of Iblis has been related to you not as a tale, but so that you may know to what the harm of pride leads. It was because of pride that he said: *"I am better than he. Thou didst create me of fire, whilst Thou didst create him of clay."* (Q. 38:76) His pride led him to the point of arrogance with respect to the command of God Most High and he did not prostrate himself so that He became accursed for eternity.

4 THE CAUSES OF PRIDE AND THEIR TREATMENT

Know that whoever behaves arrogantly thinks that he has a quality which others do not have. That quality is perfection; and there are seven causes of that:

(1) The first cause of pride lies in knowledge, for when the learned person sees himself as being adorned with perfect knowledge, he considers others beasts in comparison with himself. Pride dominates him; its effect is that he has an expectation that people should assist, serve and show homage to him, and he desires precedence. He is astonished if they do not offered that. If he looks at them or is invited by someone, he considers it a great favor for (the object of his favor). He puts people under obligation for his knowledge and in his talking about the Hereafter, he does not think himself one of them and he is more hopeful about his own affair (at the Resurrection). He fears more for them than for himself. He says: "Everyone needs my supplications and my piety and shall escape hell through me." For this reason, said the Messenger (ﷺ): "The blight of knowledge is conceit."

Truly, it is preferable to call such a person ignorant rather than learned, for true knowledge is that which makes known the danger of the affair of Hereafter to one and (makes one) recognize the narrowness of the Straight Path. Whoever has learned this sees himself far away from that (goal) and considers himself guilty. Out of the danger of his own fate and the fear that his knowledge will be a proof (against him), he does not engage in pridefulness. As Abu Darda, may God be pleased with him, said: "With the addition of every bit of knowledge, a bit of pain is added." As for those persons who acquire knowledge and whose pride increases, there are two aspects:

(i) One is that they do not learn true knowledge which is the knowledge of religion. That is a knowledge by which one comes to know oneself and to discern the hindrances on the way of faith, the peril of the outcome, and the veil of God Most High. This knowledge increases the pain (of the consequences of one's sins) and humility, not pride. But, when one learns medical science, mathematics, astronomy, language, and the science of debate and contradicting; from these nothing is increased save pride. Close to the science of religion is the science of legal decrees (based upon Religious Law), which is the science of the reform of the people of the world; therefore, it is a worldly science, even though there is a need for religion in it, fear does not arise from it. Indeed, when it stands by itself and does not call in other sciences, the heart becomes dark and pride triumphs. There is not information like examination. Study these people to see how they are. And just like the knowledge of birds, the reciters of the remembrance of God with their rhymed prose and idle talk, and their searching words which bring people to crying out, and the subtleties by which they excite extremism among the sects so that the common folk suppose that that is the path of religion. All of these are the seeds of pride, envy, and enmity sown in their hearts. There is no increase from this pain and affliction; instead, the puffing up of hubris and pride is augmented. (ii) The other aspect is that it may happen that a person study a beneficial science, such as the commentary of the Quran, the Traditions, the biographies of the forefathers . . . . and still be arrogant. The reason for this is that his inner self is in essence malicious and he has a bad character. His aim in studying these sciences and his reciting them is to assume them, not to exercise piety. When knowledge enters him, it assumes the character of his inner being, as when medicine enters into the stomach, before it can act, it changes according to the character of the stomach; as pure water which falls from the sky in one character increases the properties of whatever plant it reaches. If what it reaches is bitter, it becomes more bitter; if what it reaches is sweet, it becomes sweeter.

Ibn Abbas, may God be pleased with him, relates that the Messenger (ﷺ) said: "There are a people who recite the Quran and it does not pass their throats. They say: 'Who reads the Quran as we do and knows what we know?'" Then he looked at the Companions and said: "They may be from among you and my people, and they will all be firewood in hell."

Umar, may God be pleased with him, said: "Do not be among the tyrants of the learned, for then your knowledge will not be faithful to your ignorance." God Most High commanded the Messenger (ﷺ) to be humble and said: *And lower thy wing (in kindness) to those who follow thee.* (Q. 26:215) It was for this reason that the Companions guarded themselves against pride. Once Hudhayfah, may God be pleased with him, was made the imam. Then he said: "Seek another leader, because it occurs to me in my heart that I am superior to you." When (the Companions) were so fearful of the prideful thought, how will others be saved? Where can such a learned person be found in such an era (as this)? Indeed, rare is the scholar who knows that this trait is blameworthy and that one must shun it, for most are those who negligent about this and glory in their own arrogance, saying: "I give so-and-so no importance and do not esteem him. I do not give him any regard," and the like.

Consequently, if a person has an awareness of these points, he is extremely valuable and visiting him is an act of worship. All should regard him as a blessing. If not, it is that which is in the Traditions: "There will come a time when whoever does one tenth of your acts will achieve salvation," as though it were the fear of hopelessness; but a little in this (our) era is much, for no companion has remained in religion and the truths of religion have become obliterated. Most of those who travel the way are alone and have no companion; one's sorrow is doubled. So, one must content oneself with religion, God Most High willing.

(2) The second cause of pride is asceticism and worship; for the worshipper, the ascetic, and the Sufi are not without pride in that they consider it preferable that others greet and visit them, and, one might say, they place an obligation upon the

people from (their) acts of worship. It may be that they suppose that others have been ruined while "he is safe and alive." It may be that if a person troubles him and some calamity befalls (that person), he attribute that to his own miraculous powers and imagine that that (calamity) was for his sake.

The Messenger (ﷺ) says: "Whoever says that the people have been ruined is himself ruined; that is, he looks upon the people with contempt." And he (ﷺ) said: "It is a total sin for a person to hold his brother Muslim in contempt. There is a great difference between him and the person who gives him a blessing while (that person) considers him better than himself and loves him for the sake of God Most High. It is feared that God Most High may grant (the other) his degree and deprive him of the blessing of his own worship; as among the Children of Israel there was a man-there was none more worshipful (than he), and there was another-there was none more sinning (than he). This devotee was sitting and a bit of cloud was stopped over his head. The sinner said: "I'll go and sit by him so that perhaps God Most High have mercy upon me for his sake." When he sat close to the him, the devotee said to himself: "What right does he have to sit beside me when there is none more wicked than he?" (Aloud) he said: "Get up and be off from me, O sinner!" (The sinner) rose and the cloud went together with him. A revelation came to the messenger of that era: "Say to both to begin their work anew, for We have forgiven him who had sinned because of his good faith, and whatever the devotee had accomplished We have canceled because of his pride."

Someone (put his foot on the neck) of a devotee. (The devotee) said: "Take it off; for, by God, God will not have mercy upon you. A revelation came: "Say unto him: 'O you who, with your oath, command Me not to forgive him; instead, I shall not forgive you.'" It is usually the case that every devotee who his distressed by someone thinks that God Most High will not have mercy upon (his tormentor). Perhaps he says: "He will quickly see the retribution for that!" When some harm comes to (that person), he says: "Do you see what happened to him?" That is: "It was because of my miraculous powers!" This fool does not know that many unbelievers tormented the Messenger (ﷺ) from whom God Most High did not exact revenge, and for some of them He appointed (the acceptance of) Islam. He thinks that he is more beloved than the messengers and that He would take revenge for him! Ignorant devotees are so. The perspicacious are thus: they think that whatever calamity befalls mankind is from the inauspiciousness of their hypocrisy and their shortcomings.

When Umar, may God be pleased with him, with all of that truthfulness and sincerity that he had, asks Hudhayfah, may God be pleased with him: "Do you see the sign of hypocrisy upon me?" then, the believer must always practice piety and always fear, while the foolish devotee performs the external rites with a heart tainted with the filth of pride and conceit, and he does not fear that. Truly, anyone who is certain that he is superior to others has by that ignorance nullified his own acts of worship, for there is no sin greater than ignorance. One day the Companions, may God be pleased with them, were heaping praises upon a man. By chance that man appeared there. They said: "O Messenger of God! This is the good man we were just talking about." The Messenger (ﷺ) said: "I see the tokens of hypocrisy in him." They were astonished. When he reached the Messenger (ﷺ), the Messenger said to him: "By the God Who is over you, speak the truth: do you ever think that there is no one of these people better than you?" He replied. "Yes." Then the Messenger (ﷺ) said: "This wickedness is inside him; I saw it upon him with the light of prophethood and it is called hypocrisy." This is a great blight upon the learned and the devotees, and they are divided into three classes:

(i) The first class is that the heart cannot be emptied of it, but one shows humility by effort; that is, he is acting as though he considers others better than himself so that it does not appear in any form in his transactions or speech. This man cannot uproot the tree of pride from his inner self, but he cuts off all of its branches.

(ii) The second class is that one restrains his tongue so as not to reveal it and says: "I consider myself to be behind everyone," but in his behavior and actions things appear that are signs of internal pride; as, wherever he is, he seeks the place of honor and walks in front. The one who is learned turns his head to one side as though he disdains mankind. The one who is a devotee has a sour expression on his face, as though he were angry at mankind. Both of these fools do not know that knowledge and deeds are neither in arrogance nor in peevishness; rather, they are in the heart and its is radiance on the manifestation of all humility, compassion, and cheerfulness.

The Messenger (ﷺ) was the most knowing and most judicious of mankind. No one was more humble and more cheerful than he. He never looked upon anyone except with smiles and cheerfulness. With all of that, he was addressed (by God): *And lower thy wing (in kindness) to those who follow thee.* (Q. 26:215) And He said: *It was by the mercy of God that thou (O Muhammad) wast lenient with them, for if thou hadst been stern and fierce of heart, they would have dispersed from round about thee.* (Q. 3:159) It is from the mercy of God Most High that you were cheerful, mild, and friendly, lest they dislike you.

(iii) The third class is those who reveal it with their speech, who glorify and flaunt themselves, who sing their own praises and make claims to states and miracles. The devotee says: "Who is so-and-so? What are his acts of worship? I am always fasting and I keep vigil every night and recite the whole Quran every day. No one intends any trouble for me but he is destroyed. So-and-so gave me trouble and he saw what happened; his wealth and children were destroyed." It may be that he competes well so that if he sees some people performing the night formal prayers, he performs more until they are left helpless. If they are fasting, he sits hungry for a time.

As for the scholar, he declares: "I know so many varieties of knowledge; what does so-and-so know? Who was his teacher?" If he debates, he strives to take his opponent prisoner, even if (his words) be false. Night and day he busies himself learning phrases, words, and bizarre rhymed prose in order to use them in assemblies so as to attract attention to himself. Perhaps he learns some obscure words, technical terms, or traditions in order to overcome others and display their deficiencies. Which scholar or devotee is it that is devoid of such thoughts, in a lesser or greater degree?

So, when one sees this and hears that the Messenger (ﷺ) says: "Whoever has a single kernel of pride in his heart will be deprived of Paradise," and (pride) will increase nothing for him save pain, sorrow and fear, he will not take to arrogance and would know that God Most High says: "You have a value for me even if you have no value in your own opinion. If you believe yourself to valuable, you are without value to Me." Whoever has not perceived these truths of religion is better called ignorant rather than a scholar.

(3) The third cause is pride of ancestry, as some who are Alawis, or highborn suppose that the people are their clients and captives, even though they be pious and intelligent. They harbor this pride inside themselves even if they do not express it, but when anger appears it is exposed and shows itself in speech and behavior. They say: "What worth and dignity do you have that you speak to me? Do you not know your place?" and the like.

Abu Dharr, may God be pleased with him, said: "Someone was fighting with me. I said: 'O son of a black woman!' The

Messenger (ﷺ) said: 'Do not overdo it, for no white (sapid) child has a superiority over a black child, except when he is ahead in piety.'" Abu Dharr, may God be pleased with him, said: "I lay down and said to that man: 'Place the sole of your foot on me.'" Behold! When he realized that it was pride (that had made him speak thus) how he humbled himself in order to shatter that pride!

Two men were boasting in the presence of the Messenger (ﷺ). One said: "I am the son of so-and-so, (the son of) so-and-so; who are you?" The Messenger (ﷺ) said: "Two persons flaunted themselves before Moses, peace be upon him. One said: 'I am the son of so-and-so (the son of) so-and-so,' and he enumerated his great ancestors to the ninth generation. Revelation came to Moses (ﷺ): 'Say to him that all nine of them are in hell and you will be the tenth of them.'" And the Messenger (ﷺ) said: "Cease boasting about people who have become charcoal in hell; if not, you will be lower than that beetles who—seeing a person's feces—smell and taste them."

(4) The fourth cause of pride is beauty. This is more common among women, as Ayishah, may God be pleased with her, said about a woman: "She is short." The Messenger (ﷺ) said: "You have backbitten her, and this was because of your own stature. If you had been short, you would not have said that."

(5) The fifth cause of pride is wealth. One says: "My property and comfort are thus while you are a beggar and penniless. If I wanted to, I could buy so many captives like you," and the like. The story of the two brothers in The Cave (Q. 18:32-44)) when one of them said: '*I am more than thee in wealth and mightier in the respect of men,*' (Q. 18:34) was to this purpose.

(6) The sixth cause of pride is power over the weak.

(7) The seventh cause of pride is (having) followers, students, captives, servants, and disciples; in all, everything that a person considers a comfort and takes pride in, even if there

is no comfort, so that a eunuch too boasts for reasons of his eunuchism to other eunuchs.

These are the causes of arrogance. However the reason it becomes disclosed are enmities and envy, for every person who has an enemy wishes to vaunt himself over him. It may be that the cause is hypocrisy, for one takes to vaunting oneself before people in order to be admired, so that if one argues with someone who one knows to be superior to one, one is humbled inside oneself, but acts arrogantly so that the people not know (of one's inferiority to the other). Now, since you have learned the causes, the treatment must be learned.

5 THE TREATMENT OF PRIDE

Know that the treatment of an illness which, in the amount of a grain, will close off the path of happiness to one and exclude one from heaven, is an individual obligation. No person is free of this illness, and its treatment is of two kinds: one is cognitive and the other pratical or behavioral:

As for the cognitive treatment, is a compound of cogntive and practice or behavior:

(1) As for the cognitive: it is that one comes to know God Most High so that one understands that pride and greatness are not attainable and are not appropriate to anyone save Him. One should know oneself in order to understand that there is no person and no thing more humble, more contemptible, more base, and more detestable than he. This is a purgative that will expel the root and substance of the sickness from within. If a person desires to know the totality of this, one passage from the Quran is sufficient, that which He said: *Perish man! How ungrateful he is! From what thing doth He create him? From a drop of sperm He creates him and gives proportion to him. Then He makes the way easy for him; then He causes him to die and consigns him to the grave; then, when*

He wills, He raises him to life again. (Q. 80:14-22) God Most High has described the amount of (man's) own capacity to him, and has declared the beginning, the end, and the middle of his affair.

As for the beginning, He said: "From a drop of sperm." One must understand that nothing is or exists more worthless than semen. (A person) is non-existent; he has no name or particulars; he is in the concealment of non-existence, in eternities without beginning or end until the time of creation, as He said: *Has there come upon man a period of time in which he was a thing unremembered?* (Q. 76:1) So God Most High created earth, which is not more contemptible than he, and sperm and a clot of blood, which is bit of blood and liquid, and there is nothing more unclean than that. He made him be out of not-being. And He made (man's) origin lowly earth, putrid liquid, and unclean blood. He was a lump of flesh without hearing, sight, speech, strength, and motion; rather, he was an inanimate thing unaware of itself until something else touched it. Then He created for him hearing, sight, taste, speech, power, arms and legs, eyes, and all (his) organs; such that he sees there was nothing of these in the earth, nor in the sperm, nor in the blood. And He created in him so many wonders and marvelous things so that he might know the beauty, majesty and grandeur of the Creator through them; not that he boast of them. For, it was not through his own effort that they were caused so that he should boast of them. As He said: *And of His signs is this: He created you of dust, and behold you are human beings, dispersing (everywhere)*! (Q. 30:20) This is the beginning of his affair. Behold! Is there room for pride, or room for being ashamed of himself?

As for the middle of his affair, it is that He brought him into this world and nurtured (him) for a while; and He gave him faculties and limbs. If He had put his affair into his hands and had made him self-sufficient, it would have permissible

Al-Ghazzali On Treating Pride and Conceit 47

for him to fall into error and imagine that he is someone. But He did not do this either; instead, He suspended hunger, thirst, sickness, heat, cold, pain, sorrow, and a hundred thousand calamities over his head so that he would never be certain of himself at any hour. Perhaps he will die, or go blind, of become deaf, or go mad, or become ill, or be wounded, or perish from hunger and thirst.

(God) has made his benefit to lie in bitter medicines so that if they are beneficial, at the same time he suffers; and He has placed his detriment in good things, so that if he finds pleasure he also suffers from them. He has not placed anything of his affair in his hand, so that what he wants to know he does not know, and what he wants to forget he cannot. What he does not want to think about overwhelms his heart, and what he wants to think about takes flight from his heart. With all of these wonders of artifice, perfection, and beauty with which He has created him, He has made him so impotent that there is nothing more unfortunate, more ignoble, and more helpless than he.

As for his end, it is that when he dies, neither hearing, nor sight, nor strength, nor beauty, nor body, nor organs will remain. Rather, he will become stinking carrion at which all will hold their noses. He will become a defilement in the grave, the ambition of worms and the insects of the earth. Then he will becomes dust, humble and base. If he remained thus he would have profited and be the equal of the beast, but he has not found even this good fortune. Instead, he is gathered at the Resurrection, and held in a stopping place of awe. He sees the heavens split asunder, the stars thrown down, the sun and moon eclipsed, the mountains like carded wool, and the earth transformed. The guardians of hell throw nooses; hell roars and the angels place the records of their deeds in their hands, one by one, so that he sees all that he has done of infamous acts and shameful deeds in his lifetime. He reads them one by one and is put to shame. They say: "Come and give answer! Why did you say this? Why did you do that? Why did you eat this? Why did you sit down? Why did you stand up? Why did you look at that? Why did you think this?" Then, if—and God is (our) Refuge—one is not able to come through this, he is cast into hell and he says: "Would that I had been a swine, a dog, or dust: for they have been spared all of this punishment."

What room is there for arrogance and what cause for pride in a person whose condition may possibly be worse than that of a dog or a pig? If all the particles of heaven and earth mourn his suffering and misfortune, and the scroll of his ignominies and shameful acts is read, they would still fall short. Have you ever seen that when a king seizes someone for a crime and imprisons him and he is danger of being hanged and turned into an exemplary punishment that he occupies himself in prison with boasting and pridefulness? All mankind in this world are in the prison of the King of the Universe. They have committed many crimes and do not know the outcome: what place is there for pride and boasting in such circumstances? Whosoever has known himself to be thus, that knowledge will be his purgative. It will completely tear out the roots of pride from within him so that he does not see anything viler than himself. Instead, he wishes that he were dust, or a bird, or a solid object that would not be in such peril.

(2) As for the practical treatment, it is that one take up the way of the humble in all circumstances and actions, as the Messenger (ﷺ) would eat his bread upon the earth and would not recline. He would say: "I am a servant and I eat as servants do." Salman, may God be pleased with him, was asked: "Why do you not wear fine clothing?" He answered: "I am a captive. If, one day, I am freed in the Hereafter, I shall not be without fine clothing."

Know that one of the secrets of formal prayer is the humility that is obtained in the bowing and the prostration when one places his face, the most treasured (part of the body), upon the earth, which is more humble. The pride of the Arabs was such that they would not bend their backs before anyone, therefore this prostration was a great victory over them. So, one must oppose everything which commands pride. Pride appears on the face, on the tongue, in the eye, in sitting, in clothing, and in all activities and rests. One must drive all (such behavior) away from oneself perseverance, until (doing so) becomes natural.

The effects of pride are many: one is that (a person) desires not to go about alone, so that no one is with him. One must avoid this. Hasan Basri, may God be pleased with him, would not allow anyone to accompany him. He would say: "My heart does not remain settled with that." Abu Darda, may God be pleased with him, says: "The more that people go about with you, the farther you go from God Most High." The Messenger (ﷺ) used to walk in the midst of a group of people; sometimes it would happen that he would send them on ahead.

Another is that (a person) desires that people stand in his presence and rise for him. The Messenger (ﷺ) disliked it when anyone stood up for him. Ali, may God honor him, says: "Say to whoever desires to see hell: look at a man who is seated while another stands before him."

Another is that, out of pride, one does not visit a person. Sufyan Thawri, may God be pleased with him, arrived in Makkah. Ibrahim Adham, may God have mercy upon him, called him: "Come and relate Traditions to us!" Sufyan came and Ibrahim said: "I wanted to display again his humility."

Another is that one desires that a poor man not sit near him. The Messenger (ﷺ) used to give his hand to the poor person; he would let it remain until the man released it. He would break bread with whoever was sick or injured for (reason of) which others would avoid him.

Another is that one not do any work in one's home. The Messenger (ﷺ) used to work in the house. Umar bin Abd al-Aziz had a guest. The lamp went out. The guest said: "Shall I get some oil?" (Umar) said: "No, for ordering a guest about is not generous." He said: "Shall I awaken the servant?" (Umar) said: "No. Sleep takes precedence, and he is sleeping." Then he himself rose and brought a container and poured oil into (the lamp). The guest said: "O Commander of the Believers, did you rise and do it?" He said: "Yes. I was Umar when I went and I have come back Umar."

Another is that one does not pick up one's necessities and carry them home. The Messenger (ﷺ) picked something up to carry it home. Someone wanted to send it (home) for him so that he would not have to carry it. (The Messenger) did not permit him and said: "It is better for the owner of the goods (to do that)." Abu Hurayrah, may God be pleased with him, had put some firewood on his shoulders and was passing through the market, saying: "Make way for the commander!" At that time he was a commander. Umar, may God be pleased with him, would go into the market carrying meat in his left hand and a whip in his right hand.

Another is that one does not go out until his clothing is well arranged. Umar bin al-Khattab, may God be pleased with him, was seen in the market with a whip and fourteen patches sewn on his loin wrapper, some of them of old silk. Ali, the Commander of the Believers, may God be pleased with him, had a short old garment. He was rebuked (for wearing that). He said: "In this way the heart is humbled. Others will follow (my) example and the hearts of the poor will be happy." Tawus, may God have mercy upon him, said: "When I wash my clothing, I do not get my heart back for several days, until it has become dirty again. That is, (when wearing freshly washed clothes) I find a languor and a pride in my heart." Umar bin Abd al-Aziz used to buy clothing for a thousand dinars before becoming caliph. He used to say: "It is very fine, it should be softer than this." After he succeeded to the caliphate, his clothing would be purchased for five dirhams. He would say: "It is good, but it should be coarser than this." Then, he was asked: "What is this?" He said: "God Most High has given me a self which savors and yearns; whatever it tastes it yearns for another degree (beyond that), until now (it has tasted) the caliphate, beyond which there is no other rank. So now, it yearns for eternal kingship and is seeking that."

Do not suppose that fine clothes are all out of pride, for there is the person who likes the good in everything; its sign is that he likes it in private as well. And there is the person who shows his pride by means of old clothes in order to present himself as an ascetic. Jesus (ﷺ) said: "What is that you wear the clothes of the pious while you have made your insides in the image of wolves? Put on royal garments and soften your hears with the fear of God Most High."

Umar, may God be pleased with him, arrived in Syria wearing old, dusty clothes. They said: "There are many enemies here. What will harm will there be if you put on finer clothing?" He replied: "God Most High has honored us with Islam; we should not seek honor in any other thing."

To summarize, whoever wants to learn humility, must study the manner of the life of Mustafa (ﷺ) and follow his example. Abu Said Khudri, may God be pleased with him, says: "The Messenger (ﷺ) would feed animals and tether camels, sweep his house, milk sheep, stitch (his) shoes, and patch (his) clothing. He ate with his servants and when the servant became tired from grinding, he would assist him. He would buy from the market and wrap (his purchases) in a corner of his wrapper and bring them home. He was the first to greet the poor and the rich, the small and the great, and would give them his hand. He would make no distinction between freeman or captive, Black or white, or poor or rich. He used to have one garment for the day and another for the night. He would accept the invitation of any disheveled and dusty person and would not despise whatever was set before him, no matter how little. He would not keep the evening food for the morning or the morning food for the evening. He was good-natured, he was generous, he was good company, he was smiling without laughter, he was sorrowful without frowning, he was humble without being abject, he was awe-inspiring without being harsh, he was generous without extravagance, he was merciful with all, he was sensitive, his head was always lowered, and he envied no one." So, whoever desires happiness should take him as an example and it was for this that God Most High praised him, saying: *And lo! Thou art of a tremendous nature.* (Q. 68:4)

(3) As for the treatment in detail, it is that one look to see what one is proud about:

(i) If it be due to ancestry, one must learn one's ancestry, for God Most High has explained this: *And He began the creation of man from clay; then He made his seed from an extract of despised fluid.* (Q. 32:7-8) He said: Thy origin is dust and thy setting out is from a drop of sperm; therefore, a drop of sperm is your father and dust your grandfather. Which is the meaner of the two? If you say: "But my father is still alive!" between you and your father, there is a drop of sperm, a clot of blot, a morsel of flesh, and many infamies. Why do you not look at those? It is astonishing that if your father had sifted dirt or cupped, you would be ashamed that he had touched dirt and blood, while you yourself are from dust and blood. Why do you strut about arrogantly? When you have learned this, you will be like the person who thinks he is a descendant of Ali while two sound witnesses testify that he is captive and the son of such-and-such a cupper. The import of this is made clear to him, that it is so. When he has comprehended this, he will no longer behave arrogantly, nor will he be able to do so.

Moreover, whoever boasts of his ancestry boasts of others. Excellence must be in you, not in another; for if a worm arise from the urine of a human being, it is not superior to the worm arising from the urine of a horse. (ii) If the pride is due to beauty, whenever someone vaunts one's personal beauty, he ought to examine his insides to see what ignominies (are to be found there). He looks to see what nastiness is in his stomach and bladder, in his veins, his nose, his ears, and in all of his organs. What does he wash off himself every day with his own hand which he cannot bear to see or smell, and he is always carrying (inside him). Then he looks at his creation from menstrual blood and sperm which passes through the way of urine, in order that he may come into existence.

Tawus, may God be pleased with him, saw someone strutting about. He said that is not the behavior of a person who knows what is inside his belly. If a human being does not wash himself one day, he is filthier than a dunghill, for there is nothing in a dunghill filthier than that which appears from him. And then, the beauty of his form is not his to brag about, and the ugliness of others is not theirs to be found fault with. His beauty cannot be relied upon either, for it turns to ruin with a single illness, and small pox makes him uglier than all. All of this is not worth pride.

(iii) As for that pride which is in physical strength, one should reflect that if one of his veins becomes painful, there is no one more helpless than he. Should a fly seize something from him, he is more impotent than (the fly). If a gnat gets into his nose, or an ant gets into his ear, he is more helpless (than they) and it is feared that he may perish! If a thorn pierces his foot, he remains where he is. Then, should he possess great strength, a bull, ass, lion, or an elephant is stronger than he. What is there to brag about for something in which bulls, and asses have precedence over you? (iv) However, if one flaunts one's pride for wealth, servants, and captives, and for rule and command; all of these are things external to himself. If a thief should steal his wealth, or he be deprived of his office, what remains in his hands? And then there are many Jews and foreigners whose wealth is greater than his, and there are many stupid and ignoble persons whose governing authority is greater than his. In sum, whatever is not in you is not yours. All of (the other) is on loan and nothing of all of that is yours.

From all of these causes, those in which he can take pride are apparently knowledge and worship, and their treatment is more difficult; for they are perfection. Knowledge is dear and great to God Most High, and knowledge is one of the attributes of God Most High. Therefore, it is hard for a learned person not to be attentive to himself; but this may be facilitated in two ways:

(a) The first way is that one know that the writ (of God) over the scholar is more tremendous and his danger is greater, for the deeds for which the ignorant may be excused will not be excused for the learned, and the crime of the learned is more blatant. One must meditate upon the Traditions which have come down about the dangers of the learned person's affair. Indeed, in the Quran, God Most High has likened the culpable scholar who has committed an offense in knowledge to an ass bearing a load of books on its back: *(The likeness of those who are entrusted with the Law of Moses, yet apply it not, is) as the likeness of the ass carrying books*; (Q. 62:5) and He likened them to a dog: *Therefore his likeness is as the likeness of a dog; if thou attackest him he pants with his tongue out, and if thou leavest him, he pants with his tongue out.* (Q. 7:176) That is, whether he knows or does not know, his own nature does not leave. What is meaner that an ass or a dog?

In truth, if at the end one does not find salvation, all the inanimate bodies are better than he, not to mention animals! It was for this that one of the Companions, may God be pleased with them, would say: "I wish that I were a bird!" Another would say: "I wish that I were a sheep, slaughtered and devoured!" Another would said: "I wish that I were a piece of straw!" So, if one is aware of the danger of the ending, there is no care for pride, so that when he sees someone more ignorant than himself, he says: "He has not learned; he is excusable for his sinning and he is better than I." Or when he sees someone more learned than himself and says: "He knows what I do not know; he is better than I." Or if he sees a youth or a child, he says: "His sins are fewer than mine; he is better than I." Indeed, if he sees an unbeliever, he is not arrogant and he says: "Perhaps he will become a Muslim and find a good end."

How many there were who saw Umar before (the advent of) Islam and who were arrogant to him! That arrogance was an error in the knowledge of God Most High! Since greatness is in the salvation of the Hereafter, and that is inscrutable, each person must be occupied with the fear of that lest he become prideful.

(b) The second way is that one understand that pride is appropriate for God alone. God holds whoever vies with Him to be an enemy. He has said to everyone: "You will have a value to Me when you recognize your own worth." Thus, even though one knows that his own ending will be happiness, for example, he will not glory in that knowledge, because pride has departed from him. The prophets were humble, because they knew that God Most High is the Enemy of pride.

However, a devotee must not feel superior to a learned person, even if (that person) is not a devotee. (The devotee) should say: "Perhaps his knowledge will intercede for him and erase his wicked deeds."

And the Messenger (ﷺ) says: "The superiority of the scholar over the devotee is like my superiority over one of my helpers or Companions." If one sees an ignorant person and his state is veiled, one says: "Perhaps he is more worshipful than I, but has not made himself known." If he is a mischief-maker, one must say: "Many sins of wicked thoughts and evil desires that pass through my heart are worse than that open fornication. There are sins within me which I ignore by which all of my overt acts may be rendered without reward and within him (there may be) a nature which will atone for of his sins. Moreover, perhaps he will repent and attain a good ending; whilst I may commit a mistake that will imperil my faith at the moment of death."

To summarize, since it is permissible that one's name be among the wicked in the view of God Most High, arrogance is a kind of ignorance. For this reason, the saints, scholars, shaykhs have always been humble.

6 Conceit and Its Harms

Know that conceit is one of the reprehensible moral traits. The Messenger (ﷺ) called three things destructive: miserliness, desire, and conceit. He (ﷺ) said: "If you do not commit sins, I fear that something come upon which is worse than sinning, and that is self-admiration." Ayishah, may God be pleased with her, was asked: "When is a man an evil-doer?" She answered: "When he thinks that he is a doer of good, and that thought is conceit."

Ibn Masud, may God be pleased with him, says: "Perdition lies in two things: conceit and hopelessness." For that reason it has been said that he who is without hope is feeble in his quest, and the conceited is the same; for he supposes that he has no need of the quest. Mutarrif, may God be pleased with him, says: "Every night I sleep and in the morning I am infirm and fearful; I prefer to spend the night in formal prayer and be pleased with myself."

One day Bishr bin Mansur prolonged his formal prayer and someone was watching him at worship in astonishment.

When (Bishr) had uttered the greeting of "peace" (which completes the formal prayer), he said: "Young man, do not be astonished; for Iblis worshiped for a long time and you know what his ending was."

And know that many calamities are born of conceit. One is the pride of considering oneself better than others. Another is that one does not recall his own sins, and he does not attend to those that he does recall. He thinks that he has been forgiven. There is no expression of gratitude in acts of worship; he thinks that he does not need that. He does not know the blemish upon worship, nor does he seek it out; and he thinks himself unblemished. Dread departs from his heart and (he thinks) himself safe from the stratagems of God Most High. He recognizes his place close to God Most High as a right because of the worship—which is itself a blessing from God Most High upon him—and he lauds himself. Since he is conceited about his own knowledge, he asks no one; and should a person say something contrary to his opinion or desire, he does not listen and remains flawed. He will heed no one's counsel.

(1) The True Nature of Conceit and Insolence

Know that whoever God Most High has granted comfort and blessings, such as knowledge, the grace of worship, etc., is anxious about the decline of those blessings and fears that they will be taken away from him. This is not being conceited; but if one is not fearful and rejoices over them because they are a blessing and gift from God Most High, and not because of his quality, he is still not conceited. If his joy is because of his own character and he neglects that it is a blessing from God Most High and if he is devoid of terror for that, that joy in this respect is conceit. If, with that, he also that he thinks that he has some right over God Most High and he considers his worship an acceptable service, it is called insolence, because one thinks oneself a familiar entitled to take liberties. When he gives someone something, and there is some respect shown (to him) for that, he is pleased with himself in his heart. If, with all of this, he does not expect a service or a return, it is boldness.

And the Messenger (ﷺ) said: "The formal prayer of a person in which there is boldness does not pass beyond his head." And he (ﷺ) said: "If you always smile while firm in your own shortcomings, it would be better if you wept and considered that a deed."

7 THE TREATMENT FOR CONCEIT

Know that conceit is an illness and its cause is pure ignorance. Therefore, its remedy is pure gnosis. So, we say to the person whose nights and days are spent in worship and knowledge: "Your conceit is from that which happens to you, for which you are the channel; or from that which comes into existence from you and comes to pass through your strength. If (your conceit) is from that which occurs to you and for which you are the channel, conceit does not befit a channel; for it is being used and the matter has nothing to do with it. Whose intermediary is it? If you say: "What I do is with my strength and power," do you not know whence came this power, strength, will, and the organs by means of which you function? If you say: "It was my desire to perform this act," we say: "Who created this desire and this motivation? Who made it overcome you so that it threw a chain of force around your neck and set you to work?"

An agent is sent to anyone who has been overcome by a motive so that he not be able to oppose it. The motivation is not his but has been imposed upon him. Therefore, all is God's blessing and your conceit is ignorance, for nothing is yours.

Your astonishment ought to be at the grace of God Most High who made many people heedless and their motives have made been used up in bad deeds, but He sent to you a delivery through His Own care and made the motive overwhelm you and brought you by the chain of force to His Own Presence."

If a monarch looks at his servants and bestows a robe of honor upon one among them all, without any reason or service that he had previously done, (the servant) must necessarily be astonished by the favor of the king who has singled him out without his deserving it, not at himself. Therefore, if he says: "The king is wise; if he had not seen a deserving quality in me, he would not have sent that special robe of honor to me," we say: "Whence did you bring that deserving quality? If it too is a gift of the king, there is no place for your conceit. It is as though the king gives you a horse and you now become conceited. Then he gives you a captive and become conceited. You say: "He gave me the captive because I have a horse and the others did not." Since he had also given you the horse, what room is there for conceit? Indeed, it is as though he gives them both to you at one time." Likewise, if you say: "He gave me the blessing of worship with that because I love Him," it is asked: "Who cast that love into your heart?" If you say: "I loved Him because I knew Him and ascertained His beauty," it is answered: "Who gave you that knowledge and that view?" Consequently, since everything is from Him, conceit and pride in generosity and grace are His Who created you. But you are in between. You yourself are no one. Nothing is yours, except (being) a channel for the power of God Most High, and that is all.

If someone asks: Since I do not act and He does everything, from what can I hope for spiritual reward? There is no doubt that we have a spiritual reward for those of our actions which are by our free will.

The correct answer is that you are a channel of power, and

that is all. You are no one. *It was not thyself that threw (O Muhammad); but God threw.* (Q. 7:17) That which you have done, you did not do; rather, He did it. But since He created motion after knowledge, power, and will, you imagined that you did it. The mystery of this is very subtle and you will not comprehend it. Perhaps there will be a reference to this in this book in the chapter on the Unity (of God) and Resignation (to the Will of God).

However, now take the limit of your neglected understanding and suppose that your deeds are through your power. But your action without power, volition, and knowledge is not possible. Therefore, the key to your action lies in these three. Each one of them is a gift of God Most High. Thus, if there is a strongly-built treasury with its door firmly shut and in it there are many blessings and comforts, but you are helpless because you do not possess the key, the treasurer gives you the key. You open the door and extend your hands and take up those blessings and comforts. Do you credit those blessings and comforts to the person who gave you the key, or to the fact that you put forth your hands? You know that when he gave you the key, extending the hands was not of much value; the value belongs to him who gave you the key and the blessings and comforts were due to him. Therefore, be astonished at His favor! for He has given you the key to the Treasury of Devotion and has prohibited it to all libertines; He has given the others the key of sinning and shut fast the door of the Treasury of Devotion against them, without being treacherous with them. It is by His own justice and without any service on your part. Rather, (it is) by His own grace.

Therefore, whoever has come to know the true Unity will never harbor conceit. It is surprising that a poor man of reason would be amazed that He gives wealth to an ignoramus. "I am intelligent," he says, "(yet) He has deprived me (of that)!" He does not recognize that intelligence is the best of all blessings and this, too, He has given to him. If He had given both (wealth and intelligence) to him and deprived the other of both, it would not have been more just and perhaps that thoughtless person would complain. If it is said: "Exchange your intelligence for his wealth," he will not do that. A poor, beautiful woman sees an ugly woman with many ornaments and adornments. She will say: "What kind of wisdom is this that He gives these blessings, which do not beautify her, to the ugly?" She does not know even this much that that which He has given her is better. If He had given both to her, it would not have been more just. It is like a king giving a horse to one person and a captive to another. (The recipient of the horse) is astonished. He says: "I have the horse; why did he give the captive to another?" This is out of ignorance.

It was for this that David (ﷺ) once said: "O Lord God, no night comes during which there is not one member of the family of David performing formal prayer until daybreak, and no day comes during which there is not one (of them) who is fasting." A revelation came to him: "Whence came this favor for them if was not My favor? Now I shall leave you to yourself for a moment." When he was left to himself, that he committed that error which he regretted and for which he was contrite the (rest) of his life.

Job (ﷺ) said: "O Lord God, You hast poured all of these calamities upon me and I have never chosen my desire over Thy purpose." Suddenly a cloud appeared and he heard a cry from the cloud in ten thousand voices: "Whence came thy patience?" Job understood and poured a bit dust on his head and said: "O Lord God, it is from Thy grace." Then God Most High said: *Had it not been for the grace of God and His mercy unto you, not one of you would ever have grown pure. But God causes whom He will to grow pure, and God is All-hearing, All-knowing.* (Q. 24:21) "If it were not for My grace, there would be no way for anyone to his own purity, not to speak of others."

And the Messenger (ﷺ) said about this: "No one achieves salvation through his own works." They asked: "Not even you?" He replied: "Not even I; except by the mercy of God Most High." For this, the great of the Companions, may God be pleased with them, used to say: "Would that we were dust, or that we did not exist." So, whoever understands this will not be conceited.

(1) [CONCEIT FOR POWER, BEAUTY, AND ANCESTRY IS IGNORANCE]

Know that ignorance is appropriate for some who are conceited because of things which are not theirs and which have no connection to their power, such as strength, beauty, and ancestry. This is a more perfect ignorance. If a scholar or a devotee says: "I have acquired knowledge or I have performed worship," there is some room for his supposition. However, that itself is pure stupidity.

There is the person brags about his pedigree of kings and tyrants. If he were to see them and what their condition is in hell and how they will be scorned by their enemies at the Resurrection, they would be ashamed of them. Indeed, there is no lineage more honorable than that of Mustafa (ﷺ), but bragging about that is vain. The conceit of some has reached the point that they imagine that committing sins will not harm them and they do anything they please. They do not know even this much that since they act contrary to their fathers and grandfathers, they have cut off their own lineage. (The forefathers) would have known that honor lies in humility and piety, not in ancestry. There are also persons in their ancestry who are dogs in hell.

The Messenger (ﷺ) prohibited boasting of lineage and said: "All are the children of Adam, and Adam is (a child) of the dust." When Bilal made the call to obligatory prayer, the elders of the Quraysh demanded: "What right has that Black captive to that position which has been given to him?" This verse was revealed: *Verily, the noblest of you in the sight of God is the most godfearing of you.* (Q. 49:13) And when this verse was revealed: *And warn thy tribe of near kindred* . . . (Q. 26:214) (the Messenger) said to Fatimah, may God be pleased with her: "O daughter of Muhammad, make your own arrangements, for tomorrow my fatherhood of you will have no benefit." And he said to Safiyah, may God be pleased with her, his own paternal aunt: "O aunt of Muhammad, busy yourself with your own affairs, for I shall not be able to help you." If his relationship were sufficient for his relatives, Fatimah, may God be pleased with her, would have been delivered from the trouble of devoutness so as to live well and both worlds would have hers. In a word, there is greater hope of his intercession for his kin.

However, it may be that the sins are such that intercession will not do. Not all sins are susceptible to intercession, as God Most High said: *And they cannot intercede for him except whom He accepts.* (Q. 21:28) Strutting about in the hope of intercession is like the sick person who does not abstain and eats as he pleased in the hope: "My father is a great physician." It is said that there are illnesses that become incurable and the skill of a physician has no profit. One's temperament must be such that the physician will be able to help it. Not everyone who goes to kings has an office and can intercede for all crimes. Indeed, a king will not accept intercession for a person to whom he is hostile. There is no sin that cannot be the cause of a grudge, for as God Most High has concealed His divine displeasure concerning sins, it may be that that which you think would be less important be the cause of (His) hostility, as God Most High said: *Ye counted it a trifle, but in the sight of God it was great.* (Q. 24:15) You thought it a trifle, but it was great to God Most High. There is the hope of intercession for all Muslims, but fear is not banished with the hope of intercession and conceit does not with fear. [And God is More Knowing and Wiser]